Celtic Grace:
Thin Places

Advent Poems,
Meditations

Paschal Bernard Baute

Celtic Grace: Thin Places

Copyright © 2014 by Paschal Baute

All Rights Reserved.

ISBN-13: 978-1503203747

ISBN-10: 1503203743

Version 9.3

A collection of poems and essays

First published from 1968-2014

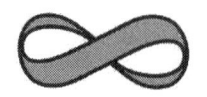

Baute Publishing

Attn: Permission

4080 Lofgren Court

Lexington, KY 40509

Email paschalthestoryteller@gmail.com

http://www.paschalbaute.com

Cross-Cultural Perspectives

"Concepts create idols; only wonder and awe understand anything." –Saint Gregory of Nyssa, 6th century.

"Our first experience with God is not with concepts or belief. It is with mystery." --Gordon Kaufman.

"The process of the desacralization of the world, of life, and of history, which triumphs today is due above all to our inability to grasp the mystery of the camouflaging of the sacred in the profane." --Mircea Eliade, Journals.

"But most of all, above everything else, who in the Bible besides Jesus knew-- knew-- that we're carrying the Kingdom of Heaven around with us, inside, where we're too damn stupid and sentimental and unimaginative to look." --J. D. Salinger in Franey and Zooey

"Jesus spoke of oneness with God, the God who is so intimately connected with life in this world that every hair of your head is numbered. Jesus lived and spoke as if the whole world was a thin place for him, with endless dimensions of the divine infinitesimally close, with every moment and every location simply another experience of the divine reality that is all around us through us, under and around us all the time. It's as if we're trying to play the piano while wearing mittens…." --Rob Bell, *Love Wins* (2011 :

"Find God in everything." –Spiritual Exercises of St. Ignatius of Loyola, founder of the Society of Jesus, better known as the Jesuits.

"The kingdom is in your midst." Jesus, Luke 17:20. Midrash interpretation: The Kingdom of God is already present for those who have eyes to see.

DEDICATION

I dedicate this to
my life parter and wife,
Janette,
whose love sustains me
through
the mystery of my life
still teaching
and
comforting m,e..

Table of Contents

Forward 7
Introduction 9
October Leavings 11
My Cancer as a NewFriend 15
Be still, my heart 17
Rain as Grace 21
My Inward Teacher 23
Advent Time 27
Oops! 31
Noblesse Oblige 35
My Heart Will Go On 39
When it's Over 43
Call Me Home 45
For the First Time 47
If I Were God 51
There's More 57
Lucky or Blessed 59
Celtic Spirituality 61
Liviing Whole-Heartedly 61
For More Discussion 64
Works Cited 65
About the Author 66
Other books by the Author 67
Forward to Resilience 69

Foreword

We are told by Jesus "to whom much is given, much will be required." It is a unique individual, a rare bird, who recognizes the wondrous gift of life and grace, and is humble enough to acknowledge whence such gifts originate and not only give thanks and glory to the Giver of all good, but live to share those gifts with all. Father Paschal's own memoirs share the life of grace as it touched and transformed him, healing him of life's wounds, and empowering him to pass that healing and love forward as a lover, husband, father, grandfather, priest, chaplain, military officer, psychologist, and pulling all that together as a storyteller, weaving the tales of his life in poetic words. That is a wardrobe of hats to wear in one lifetime, yet the wisdom in the head that wore so many hats is shared freely, and in this volume of personal prayerful and reflective poems, Paschal shares his wonder and his awe of the Great Mystery, the Author of Life.

In this volume of "Celtic Grace: Thin Places, Advent Poems, Meditations", we are privy to Paschal's mystical journey of the heart and soul, a journey into God. It is well named for indeed the great *Grace and Thin Place* within Celtic Christian spirituality is that place of divine hospitality where one meets the open arms of the Creator, and where the thin line between heaven and earth overlaps and we sense the Presence of the Holy of Holies. Paschal bears his soul in these shared lines, and it is a blessing on the reader, invited to journey and pray with him as he recognizes the activity of God in this life, on this beautiful Earth…within this awesome cosmos. All those on a life quest to God will relate to the observations, the questions, the expectations, the hope, the joy, and the melting into Love that Paschal shares in this volume of poetry.

Over the past 30 years Paschal has been and continues to be an adviser to my ministries both with women abused by clergy, and as vocation director in the Celtic Christian Church, and I have been profoundly encouraged by his personal commitments, and how he freely shares what he learns. Today, the Celtic Christian Church, with its mission to share the good news of God's great love here and now, where heaven and earth intertwine, is blessed to have among our priests Father Paschal Baute and his gifts because as a storyteller this Divine Love is the greatest story that his life proclaims. His own motto, "Noblesse Oblige" sums up his life, his work, and his continued willingness to proclaim his own magnificat (prayer of praise). With the psalmist he sings: "How can I repay the Lord for all the good that He has done for me?" These poems proclaim the good, and sharing it here, along with his spiritual journey, Paschal invites us to recognize Grace in our own experience of life, within the challenges, the sorrows, and the great joy. He has been given many gifts, and has the wisdom and insight to appreciate that and the humility and love to share it here with us. He is indeed that rare bird.

    Rev. Cait Finnegan, OMC
    The Celtic Christian Church

Introduction

The Celtic view defines a *thin place* as a small corner of the earth where heaven and the natural world meet. In such a place, one glimpses an echo of the Eternal, a striking Elegance of the ordinary, perhaps an image of some beauty, or a silent serenity, or even whispers of ghost-like voices of the past. *Thin* describes the transparent veil separating the two, like an ambiance of Something Else being present. Thin places are places where one is surprised with the serendipity of grace or beauty or a deep and profound peaceful silence. It can be occasioned by an awareness of the preciousness of the present moment.

A frequent response is an intuition of the ultimate force of love, peace, freedom and unheralded possibility. or, some new threshold never before glimpsed. "There it is, just under the surface of things: a shining, a shimmering," words of folk singer, song writer, and author, Carrie Newcomer (2014).

Conversely, a thin dark place is a thunderstorm with sudden stress or pain. This can be stunning, dis-orienting and even devastating. However, when the storm passes, the downpour stops and the clouds part, sunlight emerges, bringing brilliance, warmth and an occasional rainbow with fresh vitality.

A thin place may be simply a moment when life teaches us about who we are, who we are meant to be. My poetry, often spurred by the season of Advent preceding Christmas, or some experience in nature or awareness of relationship is about thin places.

I call thin places a Celtic Grace because this grace is found everywhere: in nature, in children, in love, laughter and tears, in setbacks and suffering, wherever the human spirit wonders and ponders the meanings of things. Celtic grace is also found in darkness and shadows, courage in facing whatever. Celtic grace is a mindful dancing to the fullness of life in all its ups and downs. It is living with a grateful heart arising from the inward journey, finding blessing everywhere, even in pain and loss. Celtic grace embraces the wisdom found in all faith traditions. It is more comfortable with mystery than certainty.

Celtic grace is not just an awareness, not just a presence to mystery and thin places. It is a *power*, an enabling, an energy to be fully present, to focus, to commit, to be engaged. It sustains and empowers, aiding a completeness of focus and integration. This ability to live fully in the present moment is well described in the small classic of : Brother Lawrence, *The Practice of the Prsence of God* (1909). Other sources are John O'Donohue, *Beauty, ( )*, and in Eckhart Toller, *Practicing the Power of Now* (2009), and *The Power of Now* (2010).

In fact, our genetic DNA has a gene or propensity for belief as evidenced in primitive civilizations. Our generation is witnessing a convergence of the two great cultural rivers of science and religion. Scientists are accepting the presence of mystery in quantum physics and dark matter as composing most of the universe. People of faith, particularly of a Catholic or catholic (more universal) faith find no contradiction between science and their belief systems. Both those within the scientific traditions and the those with the wisdom traditions are rediscovering the interconnectedness of everything. We are beginning to take responsibility for our place on this planet Earth. It is a marvelous time to be alive. Here I celebrate the aliveness and pondering of one person, blessed beyond his own recognition.

Many of my poems have been inspired by the liturgical season of Advent, four weeks preceding the annual ritual celebration of the birth of Jesus. These days are set aside for a review of the longings of our hearts, a recommended preparation time so that Christians might appreciate the implications of the Feast of the Nativity on December 25. For Catholics, Holy Mother Church sets this time aside for thoughtful meditation. I include other poems as well, diversely inspired.

This is not a book to be read from cover to cover, as if to find food for thought. It has nothing to teach or demonstrate. This is a sharing of one personal journey, a risking of vulnerability, and a grace to be shared. Each word here arose from stillness, a quiet reflection of a heart willing to share. If any of these words bring the reader to his or her own stillness, a restful pause, a glimpse of grace or some glimpse of beauty, on the unique inward journey of each person, then at some level, our hearts have connected and this sharing is made worthwhile. One circle is complete. I am a "dream-catcher," even still. Come catch a dream, a piece of your own dream with me. Please use my words as signposts to discover your own places of stillness, to ponder your own mystery.

October Leavings

Lone leaf on bare branch am I:

poised between two worlds,

bygone bacchanal of sap-rising

an abyss of mouldering fall.

Fingers of chill pilfer my green

fading to briefer brighter colors.

Winter Solstice curling

around my naked veins.

Nights longer, cooler:

sap-faltering now sires

crisp orphan.

I cling,

wondering

as stealthy nipping

weans my wild summer lusts,

wind-woos my release:

frost-scowling

asking

me

even while I hold on

tarrying,

to be

executor

of my own unfixing,

quitting home

for head-over somersault

uncertain flight

to earth's restful carpeting,

unnoticed exit

to hushed nightfall.

Sleep,

you soften my stiff

seedless form

with gentling rain

in whispering breeze.

Self, be still to hear:

the shadow nearing is

an ancient mother

conceiving for another

spring.

Fear not, let go!

Your fall was not

Rein-less plunge,

but every

curve fated,

every straying

in the due lane.

Your upborne path

is already marked--

where you land

so lightly

is cradled womb

within me.

October 21, 1986
in the mountains of Eastern Kentucky,
at a place called Hell fer Sartin.

My Cancer as a New Friend

Long have I yearned to awake

with God in my heart,

to go to sleep the same,

and to walk always

in this Presence.

Seldom have I succeeded.

Until now.

Lymphatic cancer opens me

to incredible possibilities:

it is a friend of God,

keeping me connected

with my vast inner poverty.

It bonds me

with a far more extensive

brother/sisterhood:

the ill and poor

of the world.

It allows me

to transform everything anew,

to be constantly reborn.

Every next moment

can never be

taken for granted.

This present NOW

is the only moment

we truly have.

Such grace in a microcosm, wow!

Why not me?

Thank you, Lord:

I think

I'm finally "getting it!"

February 2, 1994

Be Still, My Heart

The perfect, eternal YES

of total surrendering love

that is the Holy Spirit

expresses itself in

perfect, eternal silence.

The Holy Spirit is

a silent gaze

of God's heart, sighing:

Yes!

God silently unfolds

the universe over

eons of time,

patiently waiting

for ripeness.

Our soul is a breath,

a sigh of the

Heart of God

yearning for Love,

our love,

my love.

My heart grows quiet

becomes still inside

as I wait:

Who can improve on

God's silence?

Who dares to speak?

Just BE,

in the silent rhythm

found in nature:

Yes.

Listening from our

deepest

Self: an indwelling

Yes.

The silence of the mountains

and the flowers are charged

with the grandeur of God's

yes to us.

Her self-emptying

Compassion

is a fiery gaze

on which we dance:

yes.

I am connected

now with

all beauty,

all pain,

all mystery: yes!

My heart dances

on the still point

of the turning universe:

yes, Yes, YES!

Yes to my own search

Yes to my own truth

Yes to life, beauty, love

everywhere.

Yes to my own rhythms

Yes to my own dance.

I will dance as if no one else

were watching.

I will love as if nothing else

mattered.

Winter 1991

Nothing Is So Like Grace
As Rain

The farmer laughs as city folks complain

about the inconvenience of rain:

my favorite reframe.

Nothing is so like grace as rain

quietly or violently here

sometimes subtly, gently felt

other times a drenching roar

worth a thunderous power display

moving molding filling melting

mightily yet tenderly caressing

each seed seedling shoot

plant weed flower tree

-- each me.

Only the weathered sailor

with one eye fixed on sky signs

is seldom surprised.

Refreshing rain surrounds softens saves

soothes sorts scours scolds schools

smells soaks sounds, slakes

oppressive summer heat

washes each of my overwrought selves.

Sacrament of earth

my sister god

summon now new birth

silently surely

forcefully -- yes!

Come rain for new life

in me.

A valentine-requiem for a friend sorely missed
November 18, 1989

My Inward Teacher

My Inward Teacher

is the deeply felt "yes"

which I experience

in the presence of

an invitation, an insight,

or new awareness of

some truth to live by,

some love to give with,

some view by which

to see myself others

and my brief journey.

I have many yesses and nos

Some are self-seeking and unloving.

Some I pretend are caring

but are not.

Too often I hide from myself

and my Inward Teacher.

My inward Teacher

smiles when I give

or witness compassion

or humble service

-- which is the only "authority"

Jesus offers;

that of Love,

freely given.

My Inward Teacher

knows that honesty with myself

is the well-spring virtue

without which everything else

is illusion, sham,

mock parole.

My inward Teacher

requires silence, stillness;

finds being more urgent

than acting.

Light in the darkness,

Home on the way.

"Make your home in me

as I make mine in you."

John 15:4, Jerusalem Bible
June 20, 1994

Advent Time

"Wherever your treasure is,

there the desires of your *heart* will also be"

Luke 12:34. New International Version

The Advent time before Christmas

is designed to get us in touch with

our deeper heart's longings.

Away from stuff, from daily routine

and typical preoccupations.

To a more interior place where we

are award of what is incomplete,

unfinished, still yearning for Something More.

Be still, and know that I,

your deepest mystery, am here.

So what is our treasure?

Where does our heart reside?

In worry?

In acceptance or grace,

or gratitude and humility.

Everything I have is received.

My life stands upon the shoulders of

hundreds of ancestors who

lived and worked that their

children might have more.

We are surrounded, enveloped

by incalculable blessings--some

we cannot even imagine.

Today, tonight, this season.

We say YES to this mystery we are to ourselves.

To the fabric and weave of our lives,

to the faith that sustains us.

Yes.

Thank you, Lord

for these most singular

gifts: life...and...faith.

Advent Meditation 2008

Oops!

I walked through that spider web again.

Is the Divine Mystery

as a Sacred Spider

weaving each day

a new web of

circumstances

and coincidences

through which

when touched

vibrates, shakes, trembles

and

I can choose to be

loving to whatever

enmeshing?

Struggle we may to

break out of the web

but we are not critters

large enough

to tear Her web.

So the more we struggle

the more we are caught

and bound,

vulnerable to the bite

of Her Love

that melts our hearts.

Daily She weaves

daily we are caught--

oops!

I have given the name

"Oops"

to that elusive spider

who hides from me

and keeps weaving

that web each day

which keeps catching me

unawares.

Divine Mystery:

is one of your names:

"Oops?"

Or are you

"my-spider-in-waiting

-lurking-

still-weaving-your-web

hoping-to-catch-me

surprise-me

pounce-on-me

surround-me

bind-me-tight

til-I-am-surely-caught

wound-me-forever

til-my-heart-melts

with-your-love-bite?"

I think I prefer

"Oops."

Summer 1999

Noblesse Oblige:

My Constant Liege

Add all power ever burst

by tempest or nuclear power in

Words: Truth-fully

ready to cut or heal--still

mighty to free!

Sum all longing ever felt

by poor, lame, lost, last and least:

'twould never equal yearning

this Love must be:

wanting our free choice with such

catastrophe!

Count all risks ever ventured

by prophets, pilgrims, 'n pioneers:

'Twould never equal chance

taken when He

gave His life yet Father left;

abandoned Thee!

Reckon all love ever encountered

'tween lovers, friends, families, mates:

'Twould never equal passionate

Love for me

in a Heart that yielded all,

nailed to a tree!

Recite all grief ever endured

for children 'n loved ones lost and gone:

'Twould never equal heart

ache for me:

when from Thee to self I turn

to view just me.

Heap all joy ever shouted

for children lost and found again:

'Twould never equal tremendous

joy for me

when I turn from self and sin

back to Thee!

Take all refuge ever sought

by sailors lost or stormed at sea:

'Twould never equal shelter

offered free:

safe harbor, peace-anchor

That heart bids me!

Figure all faithfulness ever kept

by saints and Gandhis great and small:

'twould never equal pledge,

lasting decree:

Covenant kept with us,

now given me!

Relate all gifts ever bestowed

by princes, kings, lovers and friends:

'twould never equal generous,

precious Grace we

brought to earth by maid when

"Yes!," said she!

Advent 1984

My Heart will go on

Every night in my dreams

I see you, I feel you

That is how I know You go on.

Far across distant shores

and longing spaces between us

You have come to show

You go on.

Near, Far,

wherever You are,

I believe that the heart does go on.

My heart will go on.

Once more, You opened the door

and You're here in my heart,

and my heart will go on and on.

The "yes" of my heart to Love

to unconditional love,

My unconditional YES goes on

and will echo through

a universe of hearts.

Love can touch us one time

and we are changed forever

and never let go even

when the body is gone.

Love was when I loved you,

one true time to hold on to

In my life we'll always go on.

Near, far,

wherever You are,

I believe that the heart does go on.

My heart will never

stop loving you.

I could have died

from being so loved

by life, by mystery, by You.

especially *You.*

Once more, you opened the door

and You're here in my heart,

and my heart will go on and on,

loving.

You're here, there's nothing I fear

and I know that my heart will go on.

We'll stay, forever this way,

Your heart is safe in my heart.

And my heart will go on and on.

Winter 2002

When it's over

When it's over, at the end,

I am convinced this mystery we call God

will ask us seven questions:

"Did you love?"

"Did you laugh?"

"Did you forgive?"

"Did you make a difference?"

"Did you risk yourself?"

"Did you discover who you were meant to be?"

and "Did you tell a good story?"

What? You laugh?

You do not yet understand

this wonder:

we humans were created to tell stories?

Hah! There's more.

Each of us is a new

and unique story of that Mystery."

My memoir is a bid to

answer all seven questions

at once

and to invite others

to enjoy

a similar inner journey.

Advent Meditation 2013
Passage from
Resilience of a Dream Catcher, 2014

Call Me Home

Call me Home, If You Wish.

Dear God, Mystery beyond Mystery.

I am ready to come Home.

It is your love that has hunted, hounded me,

haunted me, hungered for my heart

my entire life.

It is your Love that has surrounded me,

birthed me, birthed my faith,

nourished my hope,

and sustained my discouragements.

I know, know deeply that

I am loved beyond anything I can imagine.

Loved passionately,

surely following and

tracking my heart everywhere.

I am ready to be in your arms.

I am eager to be in your arms.

I surrender now to the time and place

where I will receive your call.

I am more than curious

about this next threshold.

I trust your love to find me at the right time,

the time of your choosing.

I can never express the gratitude I owe

but I can still expend my time and energy

here doing your will.

Noblesse Oblige.

I still have more to give.

I will praise you in every regard.

Grandfather, I am still your wounded,

wandering, weary child.

Call me Home, today if you wish.

Adsum, Here I am, Lord.

The mystery of Who You Are,

finding and loving you face to face

is the great threshold I await.

Adsum. Amen.

March 31, 2009

For The First Time

For the first time

In the history of the cosmos

We humans can look at the night sky

With its billions of galaxies and stars

And know,

Literally and truly

We came from the stars.

We are the stuff of stars,

we are star dust come to life

on planet earth, third rock

from our sun, in a small corner

of the Milky Way Galaxy

We are a speck of dust on a speck of dust

In the immeasurable vastness

Of the cosmos.

We are a billion accidents piled

on top of one another, countless

biological anomalies whose slight

Change gave us an edge in survival.

Our human-ness took

10,000 grandmothers to

Get us here from our distant ancestress.

With no scientific evidence for intelligent design,

What an amazing fact

is belief in an Author of Life!

Or a personal God who

might hear our prayers.

When we consider how

we have used belief against

one another, we know how

scary belief is;

when used to elevate ourselves

or to judge others when, in fact,

We are brothers and sisters

with EVERYTHING

In the universe.

Our lives, an incredible accident

that did not have to happen.

Yet did, and ,

Here we are

Advent 2014

Note. *You Are Stardust*((Kelsey, 2012) is the book I had hoped to write for children. But I know now I could not do it as well as this is done. It makes our evolutionary miracle vibrantly real. At the same time, the story is ecologically accurate concerning our connectedness. For adults still linking with children through storytelling, such as parents, teachers and grandparents, this book is highly recommended, 4 stars out of 5. Font size of the narrative is unnecessarily small both for children and old eyes. However it is still my book of choice in 2014 for children, grandchildren and little ones in your family network. Check out the description and reviews on Amazon.

If I Were God

Musings of an ancient and

wounded psychotherapist

Were I God

I would dive

into the darkest shadows

of being human,

into profound pain,

outrageous loss,

unbearable suffering,

and I would swim

towards Light

taking with me

as much of the brokenness

everywhere and of all time

as I could gather.

Were I God I would live

in despair and in hope.

I would be

the inspiration of a poem,

the rainbow, the dew on the grass,

the color of fall, the gentle breeze,

the kind word, the tender touch,

the laughter of children.

I would abide in every flower,

every seed,

every cry and sigh.

I would be

the possibility of

each new moment.

I would be weakness

finding strength,

never lording it over others,

but in every humble service,

pitching my tent

among the poor,

preferring the outsiders.

I would nestle in vulnerability:

risking and giving Self.

Were I God I would hide

so subtly within all creation

that I could never be caught.

I would be so unutterable

as to resist being talked about,

and hate the name "God"

remembering the oppression

done in my name.

I would exist beyond any word

any symbol,

any possible expression,

but I would dwell

in every human groan.

I would avoid expected places:

some pulpits, rituals, churches.

I would never be snared

by theology, religion

or even prayer.

I would exist solely

to be given away,

never to be comprehended or

held by safe orthodoxy:

far more verb than noun.

I would be yearning for freedom,

passion for justice,

thirsting for peace,

searching for truth,

coveting affirmation,

ardor for sharing,

the making of love,

and the ecstasy of surrender.

I would be in

every form of hurting

and its transcendence.

I would be gleamed

in lowly favors, generosity,

courage, simplicity, compassion

but especially

in forgiveness.

I would be aborning ever new

in the bruised and lonely heart.

I would be found more

in doubt than in certainty

more in questioning than

in righteousness.

I would need to be

intimately concealed

because the human ego

is so ready to use Me

to elevate itself

by judging others.

I would glory in

the incompleteness

of my creatures

and all my creation, knowing

that the human spirit

I sustain

could triumph

over any human mess

and bring love and equity.

even as I do,

out of chaos.

I crave

the transforming

of futility.

Were I God I would enjoy

leaving clues, riddles

and traces everywhere,

being tracked only

by valiant searchers.

I would let myself be glimpsed

in sunrises and sunsets

in the wonders of nature,

Earth and Cosmos

in human loving

in quiet stillness and

becoming little

in EVERY human story.

Meditation 1991, revised 1997

There's More

We can only see a little of the ocean,

a few miles distance from the sandy shore,

But out there – beyond,

beyond our eyes' horizon,

there's more – there's more.

We can only sense a little of our mystery

our loves and our lives - barely a core.

But out there – beyond,

beyond our minds' horizon,

there's more – there's more.

There's no arrival, just the journey,

each step awaiting doorways galore.

But in here – beyond,.

beyond our heart's horizon,

still waiting - there's more.

We can only glimpse a smidgen of God's love,

Blink of treasures from a mighty store,

But out there – beyond

beyond our faiths' horizon,

there's more –there's more.

God's love is boundless, goodness and mercy.

Flawed lovers are we - forgiveness our chore.

But in here – beyond,

beyond our loves' horizon,

there's more - there's more.

With gifts so immense, how can we thank Thee?

By passing love on, love that n'er keeps score.

But out there - Still loving,

beyond our souls' horizon,

Amazing Grace - there's more.

Mine is the morning, mine is the sunlight.

Every day is precious, fresh gift to explore.

But out there – beyond,

beyond our life-horizons,

God willing, there's more,.

there's more.

Advent Meditation 2010

Lucky or Blessed?

We had no right to be born,]
No right to be conceived
and to thrive for nine months
without a genetic hitch,
unlike one out of 20 others.

We did not deserve to be born healthy,
Yet we were.
Each life was an accident of love-making.
We did not have to happen.

Our life is an undeserved gift.
We did nothing to earn it.
How can we argue
about the circumstances?

Considering all that we have survived.
Every moment of our lives has
been an ongoing gift,
-undeserved.

Any flower or butterfly
has as much right to be here
as we.

Do we live with a sense of
The awesome giftedness of our lives?

Each of us is another
Miracle of life who
Did not have to happen.

Yet
Incredibly,
Here we are!

As a flower is to the
Bee and butterfly,
Are we not gifts to one another?

Is this awareness
not the best gift
of the season?

…any season?

Christmas 2014

Dedicated to four who did not
have to happen but did.
We and they are blessed.
Michelle, Joe, Quinn and Chloe:
Precious Gifts to themselves and to the world.

Celtic Spirituality Is
Living Whole-Heartedly:

A Celtic Spirituality, for me, is living whole-heartedly. What does it mean to live whole-heartedly? Full-hearted, strong-hearted, etc., as the heart is the human organ most frequently mentioned in the bible. I choose to love this mystery we call God found everywhere among my brothers and sisters, *with whole heart, mind, soul and strength.*

I live with a profound sense of the giftedness of life, of love, of grace, of everything, even the universe: Nothing, none of it, had to happen, but it did!

This means that I find God's love, beauty and grace everywhere, especially in a world obsessed on the negative with nothing ever being "good enough." Because I am blessed beyond all deserving, I can never give back, love enough. Noblesse Oblige.

With this basic orientation, here are the twelve behaviors I nurture, cultivated, nourish and imperfectly practice:

1. **Surrendering** to this mystery of God's will daily, walking, breathing and living Psalm 23, living the lyrics of Amazing Grace and the Magnificat: "My soul magnifies the Lord." (Luke 1:46 ff)

2. **Gratitude**, constant thankfulness for many blessings received, the giftedness of everything, with an obligating, Noblesse Oblige, to give back *relentlessly*.--without counting the cost.

3. **Affirming**: finding God's beauty, love, and blessing everywhere, and letting others know in a world that focuses on the

negative and not being enough. How high will I soar? Attitude determines altitude.

4. **Discerning**: the great mystery of evil can be understood only by the more hidden mystery of goodness--also to be found everywhere. A vital hope comes from the struggle.

5. **My Woundedness**, that is, my flawed imperfections, all blessings in disguise, claims on the heart of God's mystery of Incarnation, each of us made in the image and likeness of God, spiritual beings discovering what it means to be human.

6. **Risking Boldly**, willing to be vulnerable, because "anything worth doing is worth doing badly," stretching my love, gifts and talents regularly.

7. **Celebrating**: living with "Yes!" "Wow!" dancing to my own music, not caring how others judge me, making every day a new "alleluia! "Thank you, Great Mystery!

8. **Self-compassion**: knowing my woundedness is my claim on God's mercy, letting go of perfectionism and constant striving, living with forgiveness for myself first and then others, and therefore with peace, joy and love.

9. **Stillness**, calm, rest, serenity and quiet reflection and meditation, breathing in rhythm with nature and the universe. Letting go of anxiety, worry and any fretting.

10. **Resilience and balance**, embracing each moment without judgment or reaction, letting go of urgency, absolutes, and the need to control.

11. **Creativity**, pushing the envelope: No guts, no glory; No balls, no blue chips—two mottoes of the down hill skier, letting go of comparisons.

12. **Playfulness** laughter, song, dance, and music, letting go of the need to appear cool, "adult" of mature, frequently finding

humor in the absurdities of life and love. I sing and dance Louis Armstrong, "On the Sunny Side of the Street," play (on my harmonica) and sing "You are my Sunshine" daily.

This is what it means for me to live whole-heartedly, discovering and rediscovering myself inside the mystery of grace, beauty, and love and service. A Celtic spirituality is a whole-hearted spirituality. 2012.

Note. I completed developing this list and posted it on the Celtic Spirituality blog on November 28, 2012. Three months later I began writing my spiritual memoir, *Resilience of a Dream Catcher*, completing it ten months later, with 28 chapters, 12 appendices, 110,000 words, with the help of nine different editors. Journaling about one's values helps retain focus. Out of my poetry and journaling came the courage and grace for my memoir.

"Twas Grace that taught my heart to fear, and Grace my fears relieved.

How precious did that Grace appear the hour I first believed!

"Through many dangers, toils and stress I have already come.

'Tis Grace that brought be safe this far and Grace will bring me Home."

--Amazing Grace.

For More Discussion

For more discussion of Celtic spirituality and issues that may have been raised here, go to an online discussion moderated by Rev. Cait Finnegan, fouornd at Facebook link: https://www.facebook.com/groups/CelticChristianChurch/.

Cait's Facebook e-mail is: caitfinnegan@facebook.com

Works Cited

Digital

Newcomer, Carried. On Being.org interview, Music link: https://www.youtube.com/user/CarrieNewcomer

Print

Bell, Rob *(*2012) *Love Wins: A Book About Heaven, Hell and Everything ElseINew York,: HarperOne.*

Brother Lawrence *(1906,)* *The Practice of the Presnece of God,* London, H. R. Alleneson. Ltd.

Kelsey, Elin, text; Soyeon,Kim, Artwork (12012)*, You are Stardust,* California: Berkeley, CA. Owlkids Books, Inc. This book is now available in a downloadable interactive App.

O'Donohue, John *(2004). Beaty: The Invisible Embrace,,* New York: HarperCollins,.

Tolle, Eckhart. (1999) *The Power of Now,* Novato, CA., New World Book LibrRY.

Tolle, Eckhart. (1999) *Pracrticing the Power of Now,* Novato, CA., New World Book LibrRY.

About the author

Paschal Baute is a Spellbinder® storyteller for children and adults with special needs. He is a "Catastrophically Disabled" Veteran, stage four cancer survivor, deeply flawed and wounded spiritual warrior who served his country over 24 years, on and off in all four branches of the US military. He has been a Benedictine monk, married Catholic priest, psychologist, athletic coach and amateur boxing champion. His Resilience memoir (2014) written for his Veteran family, uses his losses, abuse and challenges to uncover 28 lessons in resilience, learned inch by inch. He is married 46 years to Janette Osborne. They have three children, three grandchildren and one great grandchild. They live in Lexington, Kentucky. USA. At age 85 he is blessed still to have six ministries.

Thank you for reading this volume. Word-of-mouth is our only promotion. If you liked it, please mention it on Facebook, Twitter, or your own other social media. If so led, offer a word or two in a review for kindle or Amazon. *Celtic Grace* is also avaiable digitally for downloads through kindle.

You may join a community of readers by going to this blog and adding your comment here:
http://celticspiritualityblog.blogspot.com/

Other Books by Paschal Baute

These in print are available on CreatSpace or Amazon, all 2014

Resilinece:Journey of Self Discovery 28 chapters, two appendics..

Resileinnce of a Dream Catcher. 28 chapters, 12 appendices.

Inward Journey: Resilience to Walk the Walk

Celtic Grace: Thin Places. Advent Poems Meditations,

Laughing at my Perfectionism.

Did JesusDiefor Our Sins?

eBook versionis available on kindle for computer & handheld devicews, also published in 2014

Reilinece of a Dream Catcher, A Siritual Memoir.

Celtic Grade: Thin Places

Win-Win Finesse: The Art of Dealing Positively with Negative Feelings.

Win-Win Finesse, 2 volumes, with Discussion Guide.

What Kind of a Perfectionist Are You?

Forgiveness and Transformation

Me and My Shadow Self

God Overheard: Take Five! Daily Meditations for the Thinking Believer.

How Can I Make My Prayers Work Better?

Did Jesus Die for Our Sins

Where Do You Find God? Stories.?

Union of Psychology and Spirituality Report, 2015

Thank you for reading this book. If you liked it, please consider a mention on Facebook, Twitter, Linin or one of your favorite blogs. If you would like to recommend it to others, please consider writing a customer review for this book. You may offer feedback at any time by going to this blog and clicking on "comment."

http://dreamcatcherinkentucky.blogspot.com/

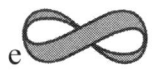

Forward

to *Resilience of a Dream Catcher.*

Whoever said life was easy has either mastered the impossible or is oblivious to all things happening in the world today. We are all born with innocent and naïve childlike wonder. Sadly, over time, life stressors and hardships awaken our eyes to the difficult and hostile problems with which we routinely struggle as a society, both internally and collectively. Nobody is immune to this phenomenon. When life throws a curveball or problems begin to mount, it is all too easy to become discouraged and adopt a "woe is me" mentality. The good news is that there are ways in which we can approach life's problems that promote more constructive outcomes. Although reality can at times be depressing, it is the powerful yet mysterious ingredient of perception that dictates where on the spectrum between negative and positive that we evaluate an experience. Just as those who have never experienced failure could not possibly recognize success, it is the challenges and hardships that we encounter that provide opportunities to strengthen our inner selves.

Our storyteller Paschal is a caring and spiritual man who exudes resilience. He has overcome abusive relationships by those who should have nurtured and mentored him. He is a blind Veteran having served his country under each branch of the United States military over a 24-year span. He is a stage four cancer survivor. His religious beliefs have been repeatedly challenged by circumstances over time. This has led to his reassessing and reframing his own faith perspectives in an inclusive way that honors and incorporates all wisdom traditions. Above all, Paschal is a promoter of positive thinking and wellbeing, driven by his calling to help others. The professional contributions he has made to the fields of spirituality and psychology verify his unique ability to offer insight into how faith and science can coexist and be embraced together to enrich one's life. He is a "Dream Catcher" who has lived in both camps. Through life lessons he has learned to leverage his inner strengths to overcome challenges and persist onward toward accomplishing his goals and fulfilling his dreams.

At one point or another we all face problems and challenges that seem insurmountable. Through the sharing of his life journey, Paschal is a living testament that we all can gain valuable life lessons from the hardships we encounter, educated risks we take, and the mistakes we make. His stories show that we can all learn to cope better with difficult situations as well as the stressful demands of daily life. The morals of his stories certainly capture the notion of "success by doing;" however, unlike many self-help or success publications available, Paschal emphasizes the concept of "success by overcoming." In doing so, his stories promote the valuable recipe of mindfulness and resilience. Developing these values is a capability we are all born with only not necessarily an ability we all develop, at least not at an optimal level. Certainly the combination of mindfulness and resilience will not eliminate the deepest forms of grief, but they are inner strengths that when sufficiently developed can help one cope with problems and navigate through the grief process. Learning how to successfully leverage these inner strengths can represent the difference between being a circumstantial victim held hostage by emotional pain and an opportunistic survivor who is able to move on and grow.

At the end of each chapter Paschal provides a passage entitled, "Resilience in Action." This series of passages is a unique resource integrated in a way never before seen in an autobiographical text. They stimulate insightful contemplation about how the lessons provided in the respective chapter can relate to one's own life. I have personally found that experimenting with them as training exercises has led to the enhancement of my own understanding and perception of resilience.

Fascinatingly, Paschal's stories capture the synergy between the roles that freewill and divine influence have played in shaping his life journey. In fact, the concepts of "mystery" and "grace" are two universally spiritual concepts that manifest as core themes throughout his memoir. In essence these are less understandable principles than mindfulness and resilience, but that does not mean they offer any less valuable of a contribution. "Mystery" represents the notion of knowing without knowing. It is being without definitive evidence to point to beyond the question of 'who or what is this Great Architect that created all the beauty that surrounds us?' Appreciating the beauty represents the actual gift of "grace." Perhaps it is the union of these two spiritual concepts that form the essence of what is commonly referred to as "faith."

Authoring a memoir can be a challenging task, especially one such as Paschal's that integrates multiple perspectives including those from a personal, psychological, faith-based and spiritual lens. The process requires a level of self-reflection and honesty that can be simultaneously both humiliating and humbling. It causes one to awaken dormant memories and feelings that were often times intentionally buried. At the same time it is an opportunity to appreciate and celebrate the happy times and notable accomplishments throughout the course of one's life.

Although I am not a Veteran myself, I have professionally worked with this population and have several family members who have served and were involved in live combat. I bear witness to the sacrifices they have made and difficulties they have faced with reintegrating back into the civilian world. I consider myself to be forever in debt to such brave men and women. Herein lies the subject matter that brought Paschal and me together; a common desire to support those who have sacrificed so much to ensure our freedoms. In supporting Paschal with this project, it became quickly evident that anyone going through a challenging time or has a pattern of getting "stuck in a rut" could relate to and benefit from his life stories.

Resilience is the stress management challenge for our times. It is my hope, and I am sure Paschal's as well, that every reader gains inspiration from his stories; that the lessons presented encourage the reader to persevere and grow from experience no matter how difficult or troublesome. Just as working with Paschal on this project has helped me to grow, may his stories and passages on resilience help you to develop and leverage the inner strengths essential to living a more positive, meaningful and fulfilling life.

Sincerely,

Scott Stubenrauch, Psy. D., HSP

Licensed Clinical Psychologist

Chief Psychologist, Public Safety & Security

Institute for Personality and Ability Testing (IPAT)

For sample and early praise
http://www/paschalbaute.comlresilience

***

Printed in Great Britain
by Amazon